TASTE THE WORLD!

POTATO

WORLD BOOK

www.worldbook.com

TABLE OF CONTENTS

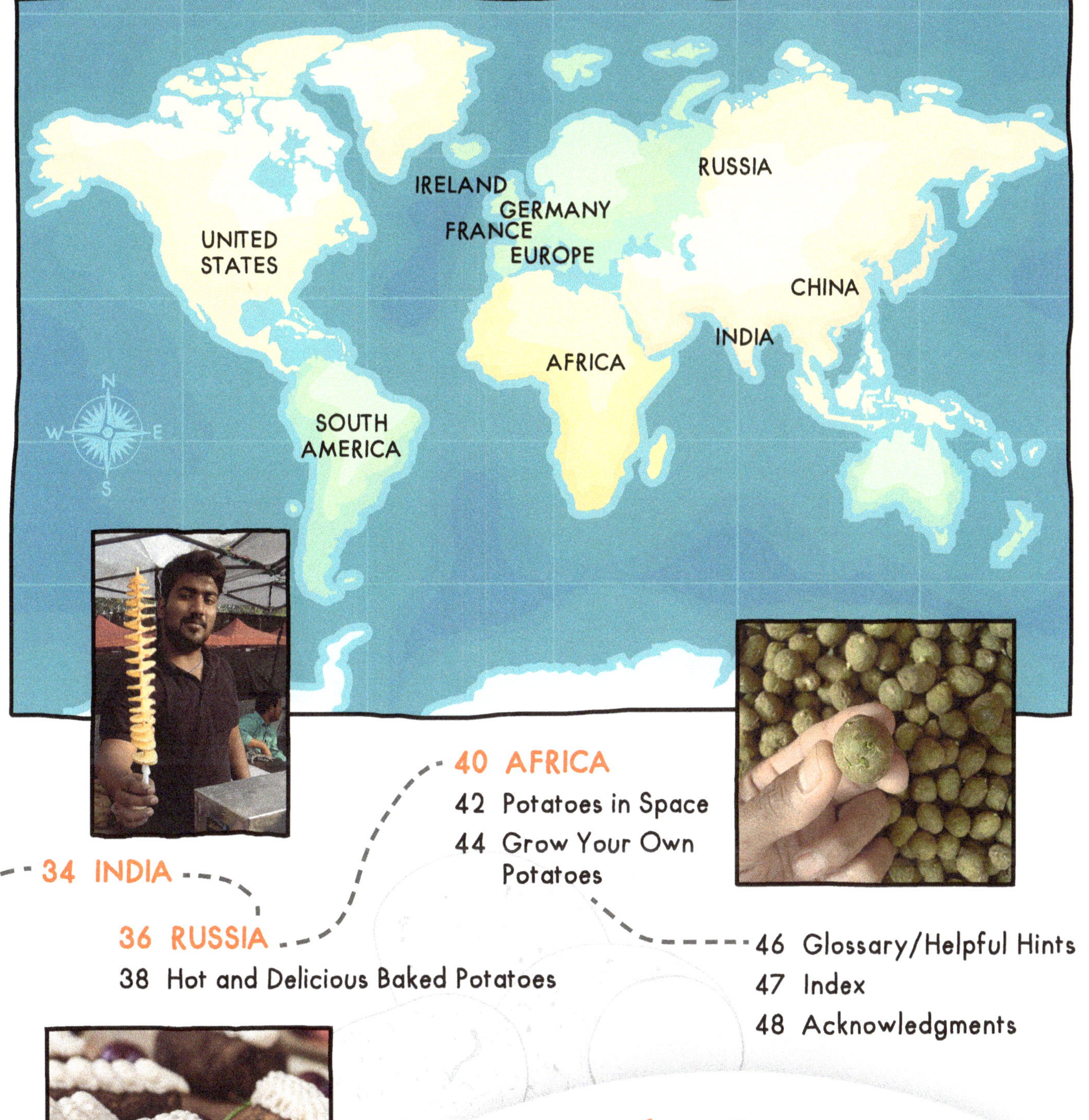

BEFORE YOU BEGIN

Included in this book are a few recipes that allow you to "taste the world!" Before you begin, look on page 46 for some helpful hints. Read the recipes carefully and always ask an adult to help—especially when handling knives or using the stove. Besides, cooking is easier and more fun when you work together!

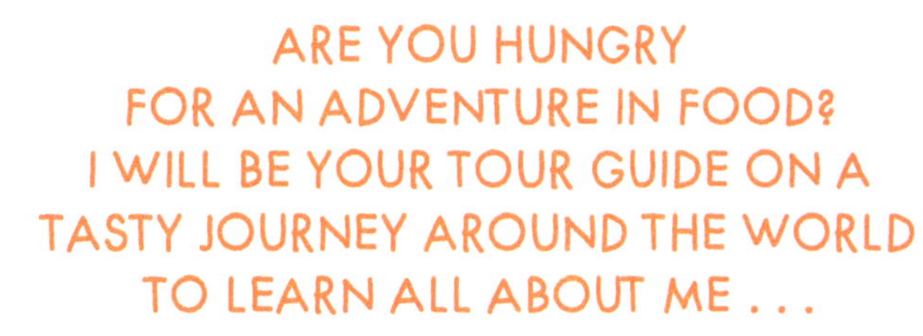

As we travel around the world, we'll explore my history, discover some fun facts, and learn to prepare some delicious recipes. Along the way, you may read words that are new to you. If I can explain what a word means easily, I'll do it right where you are reading. If I use the word many times, or if the explanation is complicated, I will put the word in **boldface** (type that **looks like this**). Boldface words are defined in a glossary in the back of the book.

WHAT IS A
POTATO?

No matter how you slice it, the potato is as one of the world's most important, popular, and widely grown vegetables. It can be eaten for breakfast, lunch, and dinner. People eat potatoes fresh or in processed form. Fresh potatoes are usually baked, boiled, fried, or mashed. Processed potatoes come in the form of potato chips, frozen French fries, and instant mashed potatoes or flakes. Potatoes are also a key ingredient in hash, stews, and soups.

Not only is the potato a highly nutritious food, it is also affordable and delicious. It forms a basic part of people's diets in many countries. Following rice, wheat and corn, the potato is the fourth largest food crop.

WHAT'S IN A NAME!

The word *potato* comes from *batata,* an **indigenous** Caribbean word that actually referred to the sweet potato, which later became *patata* in Spanish, and eventually *potato* in English.

DIG THIS!

The potato gets its
nickname Spud from a
tool called a "spade."
Spades were used to
dig potatoes out of
the ground.

DID YOU KNOW that
a potato is made up
of about 80 percent
water and 20 percent
other material? The
other material is mostly
starch. It contains many
nutrients necessary to
promote growth and
health. Nutrients include
proteins, vitamins,
minerals, and fiber.

A CLOSER LOOK AT THE POTATO PLANT...

The potato plant grows from 2 to 5 feet (60 to 150 centimeters) tall and has broad green leaves at the end of long stems. People do not eat the leaves or stems. They are poisonous!

The edible part of the potato plant is the thick, starchy rootlike **tuber** that grows underground. It may look like part of the root, but it is actually a thick part of the plant's stem! Most potato plants sprout 3 to 20 tubers, depending on the variety and the growing conditions. The tubers are usually round or oval in shape. Some varieties have a long fingerlike form.

THAT'S SPUD-TACULAR!

In 1974, a man in England reportedly produced 370 pounds of potatoes from just one potato plant!

Potatoes range in size from less than 1 inch (2.5 centimeters) to more than 10 inches (25 centimeters) long. The largest potatoes can weigh 1 pound (0.45 kilogram) or more. The skin of a potato may be yellow, brown, white, pink, red, or blue in color. Most have white flesh inside. But some are yellow, pink, purple, or blue on the inside.

SUPER SPUD!

In 2008, a farmer in Lebanon dug up a potato that was bigger than his head! It weighed nearly 25 pounds!

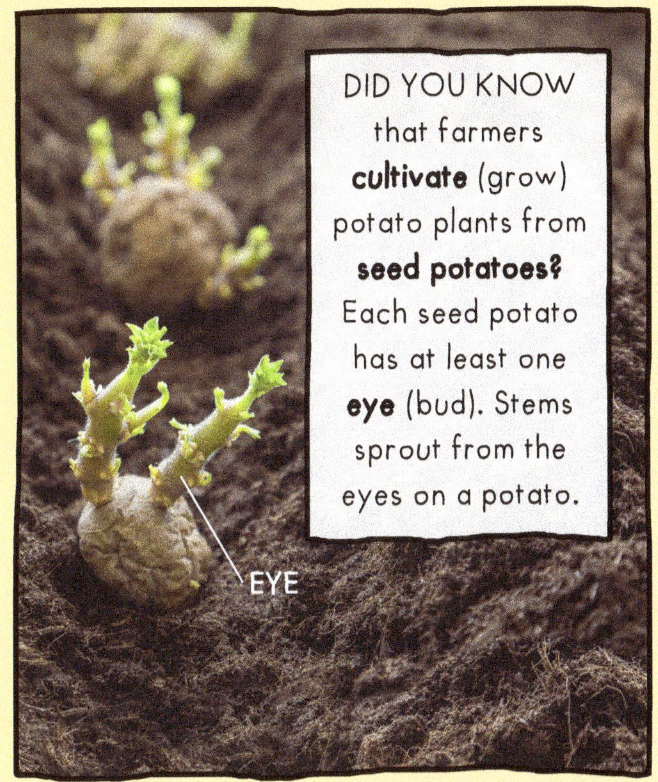

Potato growers worldwide produce about 420 million tons (380 million metric tons) of potatoes each year. More than 125 countries grow potatoes, and more than 1 billion people eat potatoes every day.

SOUTH AMERICA

The Inca people of the Andes and their ancestors grew potatoes long before European explorers arrived in the early 1500's. **Archaeologists** have found evidence that potatoes were grown in Peru some 8,000 years ago! The Inca were a native South American people who ruled one of the largest and richest empires in the Americas. Spanish forces conquered the Inca in 1532. But Inca culture still thrives today in the region.

The ancestor of today's potato was a wild plant that grew around Lake Titicaca, high in the Andes Mountains between Bolivia and Peru. The first potatoes were small, knobby, and bitter. Over centuries, people cultivated larger varieties of potatoes that tasted less bitter, with a smooth skin and oval shape.

Peru is home to some of the most delicious potato dishes. One popular comfort food is *papa rellena* (stuffed potato). It's made of mashed potatoes and egg molded into oblong shapes around a savory ground beef filling and deep fried until crispy.

DID YOU KNOW that the Inca invented freeze-dried potatoes? They would place potatoes under a cloth and let them freeze at night on a cold mountain top. In the morning, they would walk on the cloth to squeeze the moisture from the potatoes. This repeated process would mash the potatoes into a freeze-dried lump called **chuño,** which they could store for up to 10 years!

WHAT TIME IS IT?

The Inca used the potato in a variety of ways. They could tell time by how long it took for potatoes to cook. The Inca are also said to have put slices of potatoes on broken bones to help them heal.

Even today, people in the Andes grow a variety of colorful potatoes that are not found anywhere else in the world. There are many blue or purple varieties grown in the cooler climates of the Andes. The Peruvian Purple potato, which is a beautiful deep purple inside and out, is native to Peru and Bolivia. Thousands of years ago, purple potatoes were considered the food of gods and were reserved for Incan kings. Today, potatoes remain an important food in Peru, which is the biggest potato producer in South America. Some villagers still cook potatoes like their ancestors did, by roasting them in the red-hot ashes inside their ovens.

KINDS OF POTATOES

There are over 4,000 varieties of potatoes. Most are found only in the Andes. People grow hundreds of **cultivars** (cultivated varieties) worldwide, and new ones are being produced each year. These may differ in size, shape, color, texture, or taste.

RUSSET BURBANK

One of the most popular potatoes is the Russet Burbank. It has a classic ruddy, thick skin. Russet potatoes are popular both for using fresh and for processing. It is the best potato for making baked potatoes or French fries. Imagine a twice-baked potato with lots of butter, sour cream, chives, or cheese!

YUKON GOLD

Perhaps the most widely used potato is the Yukon Gold. As its name implies, its flesh has a golden appearance. This potato makes the best mashed potatoes! Its slightly buttery flavor is also excellent when roasted.

SWEET IMPOSTER!

Sweet potatoes are not actually potatoes. They are part of the morning glory family, a climbing plant, and not related to the potato at all.

RED NORLAND

An excellent potato for boiling and for making potato salads is the Red Norland. It is an extra-large red-skinned potato with white flesh. It is also very tasty when cut up and fried or for making potato pancakes, scalloped or gratin potatoes, and hash browns.

IT'S ALIVE!

After a potato is harvested, it is still living! Just watch it start sprouting when you place it in a warm, brightly lit spot. To make them last, store potatoes in a cool, dry, dark place. They should last six months.

ATLANTIC

The potato used most often to make potato chips is the Atlantic. These potatoes have a creamy white flesh. Atlantic potatoes have an attractive round shape and uniform size.

After reaching Europe around 1570, the potato caught on and soon spread to other parts of the world. The highly nutritious potato became a vital food source in many European countries, especially Ireland. But, it took a while!

Europeans didn't always like to eat potatoes. This may have been because potatoes belong to the nightshade family, which includes several poisonous plants. Many Europeans believed that potatoes, just like tomatoes (another member of the deadly nightshade family of plants) were poisonous.

DEVIL'S APPLES!

The potato got the nickname of Devil's Apples because people associated plants in the nightshade family with witchcraft. Because the potato grew underground, people believed that witches and devils created it. Many believed potatoes caused all kinds of terrible diseases, or even death.

Yet, people also believed that potatoes could be used as medicine. Raw potatoes applied to the skin were said to help ease insect bites or stings and relieve headaches, frostbite, sunburn, and even get rid of warts!

Potatoes became a popular food in European countries. Potatoes were a reliable food source in times of famines and failures of most other crops. Potatoes grow well in poor soils and less than ideal weather conditions. They are easier and less expensive to grow than traditional grain crops. Potatoes have a higher yield than such crops as rice and wheat. One acre of potatoes can feed nearly 10 people! Potatoes can also be harvested year-round in many regions.

Tiroler Gröstl—a dish made from potatoes, bacon, onions, and meats such as ham, sausage, or beef—is a hearty favorite among skiers and hikers in the mountainous Tyrol region of western Austria. Tiroler Gröstl is traditionally prepared on the stovetop and shared from the pan for breakfast or lunch. It tastes great with a fried egg on top!

DID YOU KNOW that over a billion people eat at least one potato every single day?

POTATO WAR!

There was a "Potato War" in Europe in the late 1700's. It was actually the War of the Bavarian Succession (1777-1778), a brief war between Prussia and Austria. It became known as the "Potato War" because hungry soldiers on both sides spent the winter searching for food in the frozen potato fields instead of fighting.

GERMANY

Germany is the third largest potato producer in Europe, after Russia and Ukraine, and one of the 10 largest in the world. Potatoes were introduced to Germany in the 1700's from the Netherlands. But they were used mostly as animal feed until a famine hit the country. Frederick the Great, king of Prussia, saw the nutritious value of the potato. He often issued "potato decrees," ordering Germans to plant potatoes as a way to feed themselves. But it took a while to catch on!

Today, potatoes make up a large part of the German diet. Every region has its own special recipe for potatoes, whether fried, baked, sliced, grated, mashed, rolled, or served as French fries or chips. German potato salad is a must at any gathering!

KARTOFFEL!

The German word for potato is kartoffel.

Reibekuchen, or simple potato pancakes, are a delicacy commonly found at many Christmas markets in Germany. Reibekuchen are also called kartoffelpuffer. They are made of shredded potatoes mixed with onions and deep fried. Reibekuchen are traditionally topped with applesauce, molasses, or smoked salmon and yogurt sauce. This dish is especially popular with kids!

Potatoes are eaten at every meal in Germany. People eat some form of potatoes for breakfast, lunch, dinner, and dessert. Common dishes include potato soup (kartoffelsuppe), fried potatoes (bratkartoffel), potato pancakes (kartoffelpuffer), and potato dumplings (kartoffelklöesse or knödel). Hearty potato dumplings are served as a main dish, side dish, soup, or sweet dessert. Some are filled with fruits or meats.

SPUD LOVE!

Germans have an insatiable appetite for potatoes. The average person eats over 150 pounds (68 kilograms) of potatoes a year!

FRANCE

Potatoes are called *pommes de terre* in France. Potatoes have been an important part of French **cuisine** for hundreds of years. France is the biggest exporter of fresh potatoes in Europe. But potatoes were not always a desirable food in France.

Like the Germans, the French needed to be persuaded of the goodness of the potato. In 1748, the French Parliament outlawed growing potatoes. They believed that potatoes caused disease and were only good for hog feed. The potato ban lasted for 24 years!

Antoine-Augustin Parmentier, a French army medical officer and pharmacist, is credited by many with making the potato popular in France. While being held as a prisoner of war, Parmentier was fed nothing but potatoes. To his surprise, he did not get sick! When Parmentier returned to France in 1763, he promoted the health benefits of potatoes. His clever strategies to get the French to eat this delicious vegetable caused the potato's popularity to soar in France.

FLOWERS FIT FOR ROYALTY!

Marie-Antoinette, queen of France in the late 1700's, was a big fan of the potato. She liked it so much that she wore the plant's pretty flowers in her hair. Her husband, King Louis XVI, wore them in his buttonhole!

A popular French dish is gratin dauphinois—sliced or **scalloped** potatoes. The potatoes are baked with milk and/or cream, garlic, and nutmeg. This dish traditionally doesn't have cheese in it, but you can always add your own touch to it.

FRENCH FRIES

French fries are one of the world's most famous side dishes. Both Belgium and France claim they invented potato fries in the 1700's. Historians doubt both claims, however. One thing for sure, American soldiers fell in love with the crispy, deep-fried potatoes while serving in the two French-speaking countries during World War I. They called them "French fried potatoes," which was shortened to "French fries," or "fries."

A FRY IS STILL A FRY!

Americans call the long, thin strips of fried potatoes French fries. But the name varies depending on where you live. The French calls them pommes frites or just frites. People in Australia, Ireland, New Zealand, South Africa, and the United Kingdom call them chips, skinny fries, or shoestring fries.

These oven-baked fries are a healthy alternative to deep-fat frying. The key is to make sure they are crispy and golden on the outside yet tender on the inside.

CRISPY OVEN FRENCH FRIES

Serves 4

INGREDIENTS

2 large Yukon Gold potatoes   4 tsp. extra-virgin olive oil   ½ tsp. salt

STEPS

1. Preheat the oven to 450 °F (232 °C).
2. Peel the potatoes and cut into thick strips. Soak them in a large bowl of cold water for about 30 minutes. Using paper towels, thoroughly pat them dry.
3. Place cut potatoes in a bowl with the olive oil and salt; toss until completely covered.
4. Line a baking sheet with parchment paper. Arrange the potato strips on the sheet so that they are not touching.
5. Bake until crisp and golden brown, about 20-25 minutes. Baking time will vary based upon the thickness of the potato strips.

DID YOU KNOW that French fries are a universal food? But people eat them in different ways throughout the world. They can be seasoned with salt, garlic or onion powder, black pepper, or paprika. In the United States, ketchup is the most popular **condiment** for French fries. Malaysians eat them with a topping of chili sauce. People in the United Kingdom put vinegar on fries, while the French add mustard, and the Japanese prefer green curry or soy sauce on theirs. Belgians like fries dipped in mayonnaise. In Canada, they are served as poutine—French fries with brown gravy and cheese curds on top.

IRELAND

Potatoes have been an important food in Ireland for hundreds of years. The Irish made potatoes so famous that they're often referred to as "Irish potatoes."

In the early 1800's, most Irish working-class families lived on potatoes and little else. Families ate about 10 pounds of potatoes a day!

GOOD 4 U!

Potatoes have more potassium than a banana, more vitamin C than an orange, and more fiber than an apple!

Potatoes remain a staple at the dinner table in Ireland. A simple dinner often consists of potatoes, cabbage, and meat. One of Ireland's most famous traditional dishes is Irish stew. It is made by boiling potatoes, onions, carrots, and other ingredients in a covered pot.

DID YOU KNOW that in the 1840's, a plant disease called blight wiped out potato crops in many European countries? Ireland was especially hard hit by the crop failure. About one million people died of starvation or disease. Another one million people abandoned their homes and left Ireland to seek a living in America. This event is known as the Great Irish Famine.

Many recipes call for potato flour, a flour ground from peeled, dried whole potatoes. Potato flour makes a perfect thickener for smoother sauces, gravies, and soups. It's great in baking and gluten-free cooking.

The Irish makes some of the best-loved meals out of mashed potatoes! Such specialty dishes include *boxty*, a traditional potato pancake that's part pancake and part hash brown; *colcannon*, green-tinted mashed potatoes made with kale or cabbage and scallions; and potato *champ*, creamy mashed potatoes with scallions or green onions, usually served at Halloween. Be sure to look for the good luck coin in your champ!

HOW TO MAKE SMASHING MASHED POTATOES!

Mashed potatoes is a popular dish made by mashing up boiled potatoes and adding milk, butter, and salt and pepper. But people can put their own twist to this ultimate comfort food by adding different ingredients. Some decadent add-ons include sour cream, garlic, cheese, bacon, onion, and different herbs. Of course, the creamier it is and more buttery, the better!

LET'S DANCE!

Everybody was doing the "mashed potatoes" in 1962. The dance move was first popularized by soul singer James Brown in his concerts.

Use this recipe for perfect mashed potatoes!

CREAMY DREAMY MASHED POTATOES

Serves 10-12

INGREDIENTS

6 lb. Yukon Gold potatoes, peeled and cubed into ½-inch pieces
¾ cup sour cream

12 tbsp. (1 ½ sticks) unsalted butter
1 cup warm milk
salt and pepper

STEPS

1. Fill a large pot about two-thirds full with cold water. Lightly salt the water, then add the cubed potatoes.
2. Move the pot to the stove and bring to a boil. Because potatoes can easily fall apart in rapidly boiling water, reduce the heat to a simmer.
3. Cook until tender or when a fork can easily poke the potato. Pour into a colander to drain the water and let steam dry for about 3 minutes.
4. Mash the potatoes. It is best to use a potato ricer to get a fluffy consistency. Stir in the butter and warm milk. Add salt and pepper, to taste.
5. Serve immediately. Mashed potatoes are best right after they are made.

DID YOU KNOW that you can overbeat your mashed potatoes? This makes them gummy and unappetizing. That's because as you beat the potato, it begins to release starch, and that results in a gluey texture. YUCK!

GREEN IS MEAN!

If a potato is green, it means it has been exposed to the light. This means that the potato will have a bitter taste.

MASHED POTATOES MAKEOVER!

Mashed potatoes are one of the most common leftover foods. People around the world use it to make various dishes. For example, in the United Kingdom, leftover mash can be mixed with other ingredients to make a savory Shepherd's Pie or bubble and squeak (cooked cabbage fried with mashed potatoes and meat). The Chinese mix mashed potatoes with stir-fried chilies, garlic, ham, and fennel to make Lao Nai Yang Yu (spicy mashed potatoes). The Germans make Himmel und Erde by mixing mashed potatoes with apples. In Italy, leftover mash makes a great dumpling called gnocchi!

ENGLISH SHEPHERD'S PIE

ITALIAN POTATO GNOCCHI

SECRET WEAPON!

Leftover mashed potatoes can be a baker's secret weapon. They can be used to add moisture to such baked goods as cakes and breads. Mashed potatoes make cakes lighter and fluffier. They can also thicken gravies and sauces!

DID YOU KNOW that mashed potatoes got a makeover in 1952 when the first instant mashed potatoes were introduced by the RT French Company? They were called "mashed potato granules."

Pierogi is considered a national dish in Poland, and variations of it are popular throughout Central and Eastern Europe. Wonton wrappers are not traditional to Polish cuisine, but using them with pierogi will cut down on the preparation time.

QUICK AND EASY POTATO PIEROGI

Serves 3-4

INGREDIENTS

1 cup leftover mashed potatoes
½ cup grated white cheddar cheese
salt and pepper
1 pkg. wonton wrappers

bowl of water
3 tbsp. butter
chopped parsley for garnish, optional

STEPS

1. Combine the mashed potatoes and the cheese. Add salt and pepper, to taste.
2. Cut a wonton wrapper into a circle using a round cookie cutter.
3. Place a tablespoon of the potato mixture in the center of the wrapper.
4. Using a brush, or your finger, lightly moisten the edges of the wrapper with water. Fold the wrapper in half and lightly press around the potato bump to get rid of any air bubbles. Seal the edges well by pressing down on them. Place on a sheet of wax paper and repeat until the potato mixture is gone.
5. In a large skillet, melt the butter.
6. Bring a large pot of water to a boil and put the pierogi into the water. Be careful not to put your hands in the water or splatter the hot water.
7. When the pierogi have floated to the top, remove them with a spider strainer or a large slotted spoon, draining off as much water as possible. Transfer them to the skillet, moving them around to coat them with the melted butter.
8. On medium-low heat, fry the pierogi until they are golden brown.
9. Put them on a plate; garnish with a sprinkling of chopped parsley. Serve warm with sour cream.

HELPFUL HINTS

- The wonton wrappers will dry out quickly so keep the unused ones covered with plastic wrap.
- When placing the sealed pierogi on the wax paper, do not overlap them so that they will not stick together.
- Have an adult help with placing and removing pierogi from the boiling water.
- Additional garnishes could be caramelized onions and bacon bits.

UNITED STATES

Even though potatoes originated in South America, they were not grown in North America until people brought them from Europe in the early 1600's. In colonial North America, potatoes did not become a major crop until Irish immigrants brought the plants with them as they settled in New Hampshire in 1719. After that, the potato spread throughout the continent.

TATER TOTS are an American invention! The bite-sized pieces of deep-fried potatoes were created in 1953 in Oregon by two brothers who founded the Ore-Ida frozen potato company. F. Nephi and Golden T. Grigg thought up a brilliant way to use the potato scraps that were left over from their booming French fry business. They mashed the scraps together, deep-fried them, and then rapidly froze them. The brothers traveled to Miami to test their delicious golden nuggets at the 1954 National Potato Convention. Attendees quickly gobbled them up! Tater Tots make a perfect side dish, appetizer, or snack.

COUNT US IN!

The United States is the fifth largest potato-producing country in the world. Idaho and Washington are the two leading potato-growing states. They produce nearly half of the potatoes grown in the United States.

A PLAY THING!

The Hasbro toy company made a children's toy out of potatoes. The first Mr. Potato Head toy was a real potato with plastic parts! Hasbro later replaced the real potato with a plastic one.

POTATO CHIPS

Potato chips are the most popular of all potato snacks worldwide. But historians are unsure about who first invented them. American chef George Crum is most often credited with inventing potato chips in New York in 1853. But others may have made them before. Whoever invented potato chips, we're glad they did! Potato chips have been the number one snack food in the United States for over 50 years.

THE MUNCHIES!

Americans eat over 1 billion pounds of potato chips a year!

DID YOU KNOW that until the 1950's, potato chips come in only one flavor, plain? Since then, chip makers worldwide have added a different twist to the salty snack. There are thousands of flavors! In the United States, the bestselling flavors are barbecue and sour cream & onion. Other countries sell potato chips flavored in oregano, paprika, soy sauce, mint, butter, seaweed, fish & chips, roast beef, crispy duck, octopus, and Cajun squirrel!

Today, most Americans eat potatoes, their favorite vegetable, in the form of potato chips. An American factory can turn out 7,000 pounds of potato chips in just two hours!

These slightly salty, melt-in-your-mouth buttery cookies will delight everyone with their secret ingredient of potato chips!

POTATO CHIP COOKIES

INGREDIENTS

Makes 36-48 cookies

1 cup butter
½ cup sugar
1 egg yolk

1 tsp. vanilla
1 ½ cup flour
½ cup crushed potato chips

STEPS

1. Preheat the oven to 350 °F (177 °C).
2. Using a mixer on medium speed, cream the butter and the sugar until smooth. Add the egg yolk and vanilla.
3. Carefully add the flour and mix well.
4. Fold in the potato chips by hand.
5. Drop rounded teaspoonfuls on a parchment-lined baking sheet. Bake approximately 12-15 minutes or until light golden around the edges.
6. Place the hot cookies on a wire rack to cool.

IT'S IN THE BAG!

Potato chip bags are never completely full because nitrogen gas is added to protect the chips from being crushed.

CHINA

China is the world's largest producer of potatoes. The Chinese also consume more potatoes than any other country in the world. But this is due to China's huge population.

The potato is not a chief food for the Chinese, however. They have eaten rice and noodles for thousands of years. When the potato was first introduced to China in the mid-1600's, it was seen mostly as a food for the poor. Since then, Western fast food restaurants have introduced French fries in China. And today, the Chinese people have embraced the potato. Most Chinese prepare it the same way they traditionally prepare their food—stir-fried or added to stews, with meat and other vegetables.

JUST A VEGETABLE!

The Chinese serve the potato as a savory vegetable that is paired with plain rice. This is different from other countries where the potato is served instead of rice because of its high starch content.

One of the most common dishes in Chinese households is **Szechuan** stir-fried potatoes. These thin-cut, or shredded, strips of potatoes are stir-fried together with such tangy spices as garlic and dried or fresh red chili peppers in a wok until crunchy. Then sprinkle the potatoes with black rice vinegar and soy sauce. This savory dish is served hot with steamed white rice.

Today, China is working to make the potato a national staple food because of its high nutritional value and to prevent land and water shortages from getting worse. Potatoes are easier to cultivate compared to rice and other major crops. Potatoes also use less water, produce more food per acre, and take up less land than grain farming. Growing more potatoes could help meet the food demands of China's growing population.

CUTTING UP TO IMPRESS!

The Chinese have a particular way of cutting potatoes. They usually **julienne** them (cut in thin strips) with a knife. In fact, some cooks love to impress with their cutting skills by showing how thin and how fast they can cut the strips.

INDIA

Potatoes came to India from Portugal in the early 1600's. India's hot summers and short winters are well suited for growing **aloo,** the South Asian name for potatoes. Today, India is the world's second largest producer of potatoes (after China).

Potatoes are a staple food in some regions of India, where many people are vegetarians. The potato is a prominent ingredient in many regional Indian cuisines. A lot of **curry** and meat dishes include potatoes.

Dabeli, or double roti, is a popular Indian street food. It is a type of vegetarian burger with potatoes as a main ingredient. This spicy snack, also called kutchi dabeli, is eaten throughout India. Dabelis are made by heating a *ladi pav* (burger bun) and filling it with a mixture of boiled potatoes and a special **masala** (blend of spices) paste. The burgers are typically served with *chutney* (a spicy sauce) and garnished with roasted peanuts and pomegranate seeds.

TORNADO POTATO!

A variety of trendy street foods can be found in Mumbai, India's largest city. One of the most popular fast foods around is called the tornado potato or potato twister, perhaps because it looks sort of like a tornado. This delicious snack consists of a spiral-cut whole potato that is battered and deep-fried and served piping hot on a skewer (long stick). It can be eaten plain or flavored.

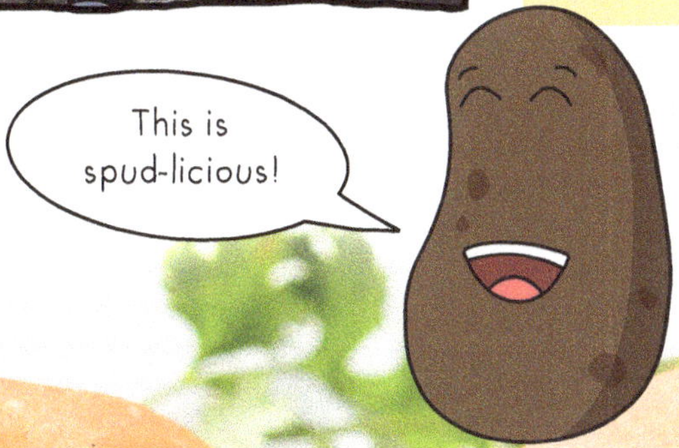

RUSSIA

Russia is the world's third largest producer of potatoes, after China and India, respectively. The potato is a staple food in Russian cuisine. It's in almost every dish! It is one of the most commonly eaten vegetables in Russia.

Vatrushka (pronounced *vah TROOSH kah*) is a popular Russian food that consists of an open bun with a filling on the outside. The buns have deep hollows, similar to a danish or an open pie. True vatrushkas are always stuffed with sweetened cottage cheese. But they can be made with many fillings, savory or sweet, such as mashed potatoes and cheese, jam, and meat.

LET'S EAT!

The traditional Russian meal is hearty. Most Russians eat their main meal at midday, and potatoes are always a main part of the meal.

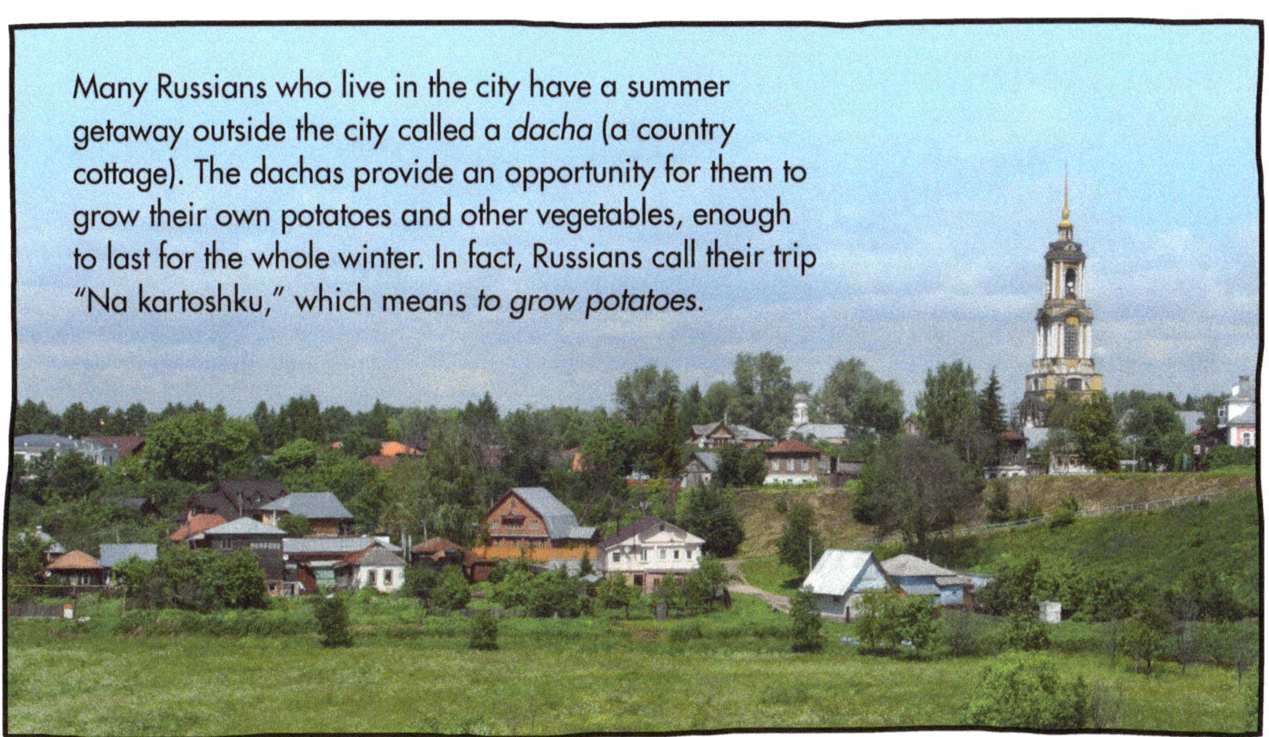

Many Russians who live in the city have a summer getaway outside the city called a *dacha* (a country cottage). The dachas provide an opportunity for them to grow their own potatoes and other vegetables, enough to last for the whole winter. In fact, Russians call their trip "Na kartoshku," which means *to grow potatoes*.

DID YOU KNOW that chocolate **kartoshkas,** the Russian name for potatoes, are not potatoes? They are little cakes shaped like potatoes. But they have no potatoes in them. They're made from leftover cake or cookie crumbs glued together with butter and other ingredients and chilled in the fridge.

CLONES!

Almost all potatoes today come from clones. That is, they are grown from seed potatoes, either whole or pieces. The new potatoes have the same DNA as the original potatoes.

BAKED POTATOES

We all have our favorite ways to cook potatoes. But baking it in the oven is the easiest and most fun way to prepare a potato. A perfect baked potato should have a crispy skin and soft and fluffy inside. When the potato is cut open, various toppings can be added, depending on whether it's a simple side vegetable or hearty main dish. The most popular topping is butter and salt and pepper. But others include chives, cheese, sour cream, bacon bits, or ground meat.

LET THE STEAM OUT!

After a potato is baked, it is important to make a slit on top to let the steam out. Otherwise, the inside will get gummy and dense.

Some restaurants in the United States serve stuffed baked potatoes. The insides are scooped out and mixed with cheese, meat, chili, or broccoli. The mixture is then returned to the potato shell and served as a "twice baked" or "loaded" baked potato. Many places, such as the United Kingdom, refer to a baked potato as a "jacket potato." The British use very different toppings, such as baked beans and tuna salad. In Turkey, toppings include sweet corn, sausage, mushrooms, or carrots.

Hasselback potatoes are a type of baked potato said to have originated in 1953 at a restaurant in Sweden called the Hasselbacken. These fancy potatoes are peeled and cut halfway through in very thin, crosswise slices that fan out slightly like an accordion.

CHEESY HASSELBACK POTATOES

Makes 4 servings

INGREDIENTS

4 medium Russet potatoes
2 tbsp. olive oil
salt and pepper

10 to 14 thin slices cheddar cheese, cut into 1-inch squares
⅓ cup shredded Parmesan cheese

STEPS

1. Line a baking sheet with aluminum foil. Preheat the oven to 450 °F (232 °C).
2. Place a potato between two wooden chopsticks and carefully cuts slices into the potato every ⅛ inch. Do not cut all the way through the potato. Repeat this step with the other potatoes.
3. Place potatoes on baking sheet about 2 inches apart and brush them with olive oil, letting some oil go between the slices. Season them with salt and pepper, to taste. Bake them for 55-60 minutes or until tender.
4. Remove the potatoes from the oven; with two forks, open the slices slightly so that you can insert a piece of cheese between each slice. Because the potato is very hot, be careful when doing this step. Sprinkle the tops of the potatoes with some Parmesan cheese, then return them to the oven and continue baking until the cheese is melted, about 3 minutes.
5. Remove the potatoes from the oven and serve immediately.

PERFECT HAND WARMERS!

Back in the horse-and-buggy days, people put hot baked potatoes in their coat pockets to keep their hands warm in cold weather. The potatoes could be eaten later as a snack!

AFRICA

The potato arrived in Africa around the 1800's, and early 1900's in some cases. Africa's highlands are well suited for growing potatoes. Regions of Southern Africa and North Africa also grow potatoes well during the cooler winter months.

Potato production in Africa more than tripled beginning in the mid-1990's. Today, in some African countries, production continues to expand rapidly. Algeria and Egypt are the top potato-producing countries in Africa. Potatoes are cultivated in small household gardens to big commercial farms.

IT'S A HEALER!

The African wild potato is a plant that's used to make medicine. People throughout South Africa use this bitter plant as an herbal supplement for its healing benefits. It is also said to prevent storms and fight off nightmares!

DID YOU KNOW that in South Africa a favorite thing to do on a Sunday afternoon is to have a braai? A braai (pronounced "bry," like "cry") is similar to a barbecue or picnic. Family and friends gather to enjoy a meal of grilled meats and side dishes. A braai is not complete without a big bowl of potato salad! An alternative side dish could be a creamy potato bake made with layers of sliced potatoes and caramelized onions and topped with Parmesan cheese.

Traditional cooking in North Africa involves the use of a **tagine,** especially in Morocco. A tagine refers to both a cooking and serving dish as well as the meal prepared in it. The serving dish consists of a wide, shallow ceramic or clay dish, with a cone-shaped lid. Most tagine recipes involve layering onion slices across the bottom as a bed for the other ingredients, such as meats, vegetables, and spices. In the case of the flavorful Moroccan fish tagine, potato slices are layered over the onions along with the fish, vegetables, and spices.

POTATOES IN SPACE

In 1995, potatoes became the first vegetable to be grown in space! American astronauts aboard the American space shuttle Columbia grew five small potatoes in orbit from tiny, marble-sized seed potatoes called minitubers.

WHY POTATOES?

The National Aeronautics and Space Administration (NASA), the U.S. space agency, helped develop technology to grow potatoes in space. The goal is to be able to feed astronauts during long space missions.

NASA also wants to grow potatoes on Mars! Since the potato is so easy to grow, NASA scientists aim to prove that it can grow just about anywhere, even in the cold, dry conditions on Mars. This might seem like something out of this world to you now, but it could be a real possibility in the not-too-distant future. NASA has set a goal of sending people to Mars by the 2030's.

Scientists reported good results from a potato-growing experiment titled "Potatoes on Mars." They recreated the harsh conditions on the Red Planet with soil from a Peruvian desert in a box, planted a potato, sealed up the box, and eventually a potato plant emerged!

DID YOU KNOW that growing potatoes on Mars was the subject of a motion picture? The fictional movie, *The Martian* (2015), is about an American plant scientist-turned-astronaut who gets stranded on Mars with only limited supplies, including a few potatoes. The character survives by growing enough potatoes to feed himself until he is rescued.
Take me to your leader!

GROW YOUR OWN
POTATOES!

Growing your own potatoes can be a lot of fun, and it's easy. All you need is the right container, good soil, and a sunny location that will get 6 to 8 hours of sunlight.

Since potatoes grow below the soil surface, you will need to choose a large, deep container, such as a 5-gallon bucket. The deeper, the better because you will be adding soil as the spud sprouts and grows. Be sure there are drainage holes in the bottom of the container.

Choose quick growing seed potatoes. To avoid overcrowding, remove some of the shoots, leaving only 2 to 3 shoots per plant.

Fill the container with 4 inches (10 centimeters) of potting soil. Place 3 to 4 seed potatoes on top with lots of space in-between. The shoots should be pointing up. Cover the potatoes with 4 to 6 inches (10 to 15 centimeters) of potting soil and water well. When the shoots grow 4 inches above the soil surface, cover them up with potting soil, leaving just the tops of the foliage poking through. Continue this layering process until the top of the container is reached. Keep the soil moist but not wet. A wet soil can cause the potatoes to rot. The addition of fertilizer is beneficial; follow the directions on the package.

The potatoes will be ready to harvest after the plant flowers. Stop watering once the stems turn yellow and the plant is beginning to die down. Wait a few days and then tip the container over to reveal your harvest. Remove all the dirt from them, and allow them to dry in a cool, dry place for a few days before storing them.

DID YOU KNOW that if potatoes get stressed out, they will grow into funny shapes? Long, dry periods of hot temperatures over 90 °F (32 °C) and inconsistent watering will result in odd shapes. When the soil moisture dries out, the potato stops growing. The potato will start a new section of tuber when the soil regains its moisture. That is why a potato will look funny!

CELEBRATE THE POTATO!

August 19 is National Potato Day in the United States.

Looks aren't everything!

GLOSSARY

aloo *(AH loo)* The South Asian name for potato.

archaeologist *(AHR kee OL uh jihst)* A person who studies the people, customs, and life of ancient times.

chuño *(CHOO nyoh)* Potatoes frozen by exposure, thawed, and dried, forming the chief vegetable food of Indians of Bolivia and Peru.

condiment *(KON duh muhnt)* Something used to give flavor and relish to food.

cuisine *(kwih ZEEN)* A style of cooking or preparing food.

cultivar *(KUHL tuh vahr)* A variety produced by selective breeding.

cultivate *(KUHL tuh vayt)* To help plants grow by plowing, weeding, and planting seeds, and then caring for the plants.

curry *(KUR ee)* A peppery sauce made from a mixture of spices, seeds, and turmeric. Curry is a popular seasoning in India.

eye The little buds on potatoes from which a sprout can grow.

indigenous *(ihn DIHJ uh nuhs)* Native to a region.

julienne *(JOO lee EHN)* Cut in thin strips or small pieces: julienne potatoes.

kartoshka *(kahr TOSH kah)* The Russian name for potato.

masala *(mah SAH lah)* A blend of spices used in Indian cooking.

scallop *(SKOL uhp or SKAL uhp)* To bake with sauce and breadcrumbs in a dish.

seed potato A whole potato or cut pieces of potatoes used for cultivating potato plants.

Szechuan *(SEHCH won)* Of or relating to a style of Chinese cooking, noted as especially sweet-smelling and spicy.

tagine *(tah ZHEEN)* Refers to a type of North African cookware and a stew of spiced meat and vegetables slow-cooked in a shallow clay or ceramic dish with a cone-shaped lid.

tuber *(TOO buhr)* Potato; the solid, thick, edible part of an underground stem.

HELPFUL HINTS

When working in the kitchen with food, keep these helpful hints in mind to make sure your work goes smoothly and safely. Then enjoy the tasty treats you make!

- **Wash your hands** before you begin food preparation and after you've touched raw eggs or meat.
- Thoroughly **wash fruits and vegetables.**
- **Use oven mitts** when handling hot pots, pans, or trays.
- **Have an adult help** when working with knives and hot stoves or ovens.

INDEX

World Book, Inc.
180 North LaSalle Street
Suite 900
Chicago, Illinois 60601
USA

For information about other "Taste the World!" titles, as well as other World Book print and digital publications, please go to www.worldbook.com.

For information about other World Book publications, call 1-800-WORLDBK (967-5325).

For information about sales to schools and libraries, call 1-800-975-3250 (United States) or 1-800-837-5365 (Canada).

Library of Congress Cataloging-in-Publication Data

Title: Potato.
Description: Chicago, Illinois: World Book Inc., 2020. | Series: Taste the world! | Includes index.
Identifiers: LCCN 2019037382 | ISBN 9780716628620 (hardcover)
Subjects: LCSH: Cooking (Potatoes) | Potatoes.
Classification: LCC TX803.P8 P59 2020 | DDC 641.6/521--dc23
LC record available at https://lccn.loc.gov/2019037382

Taste the World!
ISBN: 978-0-7166-2858-3 (set, hc.)

Potato
ISBN: 978-0-7166-2862-0 (hc.)

Also available as:
ISBN: 978-0-7166-2870-5 (e-book)

2nd printing July 2020

STAFF

Editorial

Writer: Mellonee Carrigan

Manager, New Product Development
Nick Kilzer

Proofreader: Nathalie Strassheim

Manager, Contracts and Compliance
(Rights and Permissions): Loranne K. Shields

Manager, Indexing Services
David Pofelski

Digital

Director, Digital Product Development
Erika Meller

Digital Product Manager
Jonathan Wills

Graphics and Design

Coordinator, Design Development
and Production
Brenda Tropinski

Senior Visual Communications Designer
Melanie Bender

Media Editor: Rosalia Bledsoe

Senior Web Designer/Digital Media Developer
Matt Carrington

Manufacturing/Production

Manufacturing Manager: Anne Fritzinger

Production Specialist: Curley Hunter

ACKNOWLEDGMENTS

Cover   © Nils Z, Shutterstock; © The Crimson Monkey/iStockphoto
Character artwork by Matthew Carrington
2-3   © Shutterstock; *Antoine Parmentier* (1812), oil on canvas by François Dumont; Palace of Versailles; © KF Biotech
4-9   © Shutterstock
10-11   Public Domain; © Byelikova Oksana, Shutterstock; © Balinda/Shutterstock; © Ildi Papp, Shutterstock
12-13   © Poleij Photo/Shutterstock; © Tiger Images/Shutterstock; © Billion Photos/Shutterstock; © Hong Vo, Shutterstock; SASA © Crown Copyright
14-15   © Nattika/Shutterstock; © Tina Bumann, age footstock; © Rodrigo Bark, Shutterstock
16-17   © Ildi Papp, Shutterstock; © ullstein bild/Getty Images
18-19   *Antoine Parmentier* (1812), oil on canvas by François Dumont; Palace of Versailles; © Liliya Kandrashevich, Shutterstock
20-21   © Tatyaby/Shutterstock
22-23   © Free Skyline/Shutterstock; © PJ Photography/Shutterstock; © Simon Reddy, Alamy Images
24-25   © Foodio/Shutterstock
26-27   © Korneeva Kristina, Shutterstock; © GM Vozd/iStockphoto; © Elena Shashkina, Shutterstock; © The French's Food Company; © Brent Hofacker, Shutterstock
28-29   © The Crimson Monkey/iStockphoto; © Nicescene/Shutterstock; © Archivist/Adobe Stock
30-31   © Jiri Hera, Shutterstock; © Teresa Ambra
32-33   © Andrey Starostin, Shutterstock; © Frederic J. Brown, AFP/Getty Images
34-35   © Anil Ghawana, Alamy Images; © Indian Food Images/Shutterstock; © Reddees/Shutterstock
36-37   © Yelena Strokin, age footstock; © Rogkoff/iStockphoto; © Ekaterina Smirnova, Shutterstock
38-39   © Paul Fourie, Shutterstock; © Alp Aksoy, Shutterstock; © Rimma Bondarenko, Shutterstock; WORLD BOOK photo by Rosalia Bledsoe
40-41   © Hansie Oosthuizen, Shutterstock; © Konstantin Kopachinsky, Shutterstock
42-43   © KF Biotech; © Twentieth Century Fox
44-45   © Shutterstock